S0-ASL-605

LET'S TALK ABOUT

Keeping Safe

WITHDRAWN

Sarah Levete

Mount Laurel Library
100 Walt Whitman Avenue
Mount Laurel, NJ 08054-9539
856-234-7319
www.mtlaurel.lib.nj.us

Stargazer Books

© Aladdin Books Ltd 2007

Designed and produced by
Aladdin Books Ltd

First published in the
United States in 2007 by
Stargazer Books
c/o The Creative Company
123 South Broad Street
P.O. Box 227
Mankato, Minnesota 56002

All rights reserved
Printed in the United States

Design: Simon Morse; Flick, Book
Design and Graphics

Picture Research:
Alexa Brown

Editor: Rebecca Pash

The consultant, Kate Challis, is
Resources & Projects Coordinator
at the Suzy Lamplugh Trust. We
would like to thank Kate for
assisting with the personal
safety sections in this book.

*Library of Congress Cataloging- in-
Publication Data*

Levete, Sarah.
    Keeping safe / by Sarah Levete.
       p. cm. -- (Let's talk about)
    Includes index.
    ISBN 978-1-59604-088-5
    1. Safety education--Juvenile
literature. 2. Children and strangers--
Juvenile literature. 3. Internet and
children--Juvenile literature. 4. Bullying--
Juvenile literature. I. Title. II. Let's talk
about (Stargazer Books (Firm))

HQ770.7.L48 2006
613.6--dc22

                              2005057641

Contents

"Why should we talk about safety?"

All around, there are rules to protect you from harm, such as having to wear a seatbelt in a car. There are also warnings that alert you to dangers, such as a red light at a road crossing.

Dangerous situations are uncommon but they can happen at any time, and anywhere—at home, at school, in the street, even playing on the computer.

There are lots of ways that you can make sure you stay safe and happy.

As you grow up, you are allowed to do things you may not have done before. If you are aware of the possible dangers, you can take steps to stay safe. This book discusses what you can do to avoid or deal with tricky situations that may arise. You will discover that talking about safety is an important way of being prepared and keeping safe.

"How can I stay safe?"

Before you go anywhere, think about where you are going and how you are going to get there. If you are prepared, you will be more in control and able to avoid or deal with difficult situations.

Talk to your parents or carers about places you should avoid and always let them know where you are going, even if it's just outside to play.

Always let a grown-up know where you are going and when you are due back.

Did you know...

Do you know your home phone number? It's a good idea to learn it or write it on your hand when you are out so that you can phone home if necessary. Learn how to make a collect call, and what number to dial in an emergency.

Walk tall. If you look confident, others are less likely to trouble you. Pay attention to what is going on around you—if you see trouble ahead, you can take steps to avoid it.

"Am I safe at home?"

Home is a place of safety and security. But accidents can happen at home—and they are often easy to avoid. It's easy to trip over toys left lying around, to slip on a wet bathroom floor, or to touch a hot stove. Accidents can often be prevented if you are aware of possible dangers.

Soap and water are easy to slip on—keep them in the bath and not on the floor.

Talk to your parent or carer about things you shouldn't do alone and the reasons why. For instance, it's great to help in the kitchen, but you need to watch out for boiling water, hot ovens, and sharp knives.

Think about it

These are just some of the things to be aware of at home:

• Never play with matches. Fire spreads quickly. Talk to your parents or carers about fire risks, and discuss what to do in the case of a fire.

• Only take medicine prescribed for you, or given to you by your parent or carer.

• Electricity can be dangerous—never touch anything electrical, such as sockets, especially if you have wet hands.

"What if I'm at home alone?"

Ask your parents or carers to put a list of important phone numbers by the phone. These may be the numbers of their cell phones, the police, relatives, or a trusted neighbor. If you feel worried by anything, call one of the people on the list and ask them to come and get you.

Calling an emergency service, such as the fire department, is always free.

In an emergency, call the emergency services. Stay calm. Give your address and phone number. In case of a fire, get out first, and then call from a neighbor's house or a public phone. Never try to deal with a fire yourself.

Did you know…

If you are at home without a grown-up, remember these important rules:

• Don't say that you are alone if you answer the phone. Say something like "Mom can't come to the phone right now" instead of "Mom isn't here."

• Don't answer the door—whoever is there will come back if it's important. No one will think you are rude. Call the police if the person doesn't go away.

"Why should I take care when having fun?"

There are lots of fun things to do at home, such as playing on the computer or watching television. But your fun can be spoiled if you come across something you find upsetting or frightening.

The Internet is fantastic for finding out things. But it is easy to access websites you don't want to by mistake. Talk to your parents or carers and agree on which sites you will be visiting.

Agree what you can do on the Internet to avoid logging on to upsetting websites.

It is fun to watch movies with friends, but be aware of the age rating—it is there to prevent you seeing things you may find frightening or upsetting. Let an adult know what you will be watching and never let friends force you into watching something you don't want to.

Did you know...

Computer games have age ratings, just like movies. This isn't to stop you having fun—it's to make sure that the games are suitable for your age so you can enjoy them. Let someone know if you come across something frightening or upsetting.

"Is it ok to make friends on the Internet?"

You can make friends on the Internet, but be aware that some people are not truthful about who they are.

You may "meet" new friends in "chatrooms" on the Internet. This is great but, because you cannot see the person, you must be cautious. There is no way of telling if a person you make friends with is being truthful about their age, or even if he or she is a boy or girl!

If you ever receive unpleasant messages or threats, leave the "chatroom" and tell your parent or carer.

Did you know…

Always follow these guidelines for Internet use:

• Never tell anyone your full name, your address, your home or cell-phone number, or even your school.

• Never tell anyone your password. If you think someone knows it, change it. It's a good idea to change it regularly.

• If you arrange to meet someone, tell your parent or carer. Arrange to meet in a busy place and make sure your parent or carer knows where you are and when you are due home. If possible, go with a responsible adult.

"Where can I go to play safely?"

Whenever you go out, even if it's to play outside your house, tell a parent or carer who you are with and where you are going. It's better to play in busy, open spaces such as a playground or park instead of dark, isolated places. Busy roads, railroads, and building sites are very dangerous and should be avoided.

Busy parks and playgrounds are great places to play safely.

Think about it

Wear the correct safety gear for the activity you are doing. It's cooler to be safe than to end up in a hospital with a broken bone!

If you are near water, make sure you stay well back. Water can be unpredictable and it's easy to get into serious difficulty, even if it's a small stream.

Wherever you are, think about where you could go to find help if something went wrong. If you are with others, arrange a place to meet in case you get separated.

"How should I deal with strangers?"

At first, everyone is a stranger! Most strangers are very pleasant, but you can't tell this just by looking at someone. It's best to be cautious, however nice someone may seem. Never accept rides or treats from people unless your parents or carers have said it's ok. Ask your parents or carers who can give you a ride.

Never accept a ride unless your parent or carer has said it's ok.

My Story

"A lady who lives on my street offered me a ride. I felt silly, but I said I'd wait for the bus. When I told Dad later, he said I was right to refuse the ride. Dad's now made a list of people who can give me a ride, and that includes the lady from our street." Ellie

Be polite, but firm. No one will think you are rude. If you feel in danger, shout for help. It's important to tell your parent or carer if a stranger offers you a ride or presents, or if there is a stranger with whom you are becoming friendly.

"What do I do if there's a problem?"

Trust your feelings and never think, "I'm just being silly." If anything makes you feel unsafe, walk away and tell an adult. You're not a sissy or being rude. If something goes wrong, go to a busy place such as a store, or a gas or police station, and ask an assistant for help.

Walk away from anything or anyone who makes you feel unsafe.

If you ever feel in danger, shout very loudly for help or for someone to call the police. If you see something suspicious, tell someone. No one will be angry with you. You could prevent someone else from getting hurt.

Think about it

Imagine you and your dad are shopping on a busy Saturday. You get separated. Do you...

A) Find a store assistant who can phone the police?

B) Go off with a stranger who offers to take you home?

C) Look for your dad on your own?

D) Sit down and wait?

Answer: A. Talk to your parents or carers about why A is the correct answer.

"What if something doesn't feel right?"

Secrets about birthday parties or presents are fun! But some secrets don't feel right or safe. No one should ask you to keep a secret about being touched or hurt. If this happens, tell a grown-up you trust. Hugs and cuddles are meant to make you feel safe and loved. They should never be secret.

Hugs should make you feel safe and happy. They should never be secret.

If someone touches you or talks to you in a way that makes you feel unsafe or uncomfortable, tell an adult you trust. Even if the person involved is someone you know well, such as a relative or a babysitter, it is not right if they make you feel uncomfortable. Trust your feelings and remember, you haven't done anything wrong.

My Story

"My mom's friend made me sit on his knee. It felt wrong and creepy. He said it was our secret, but I didn't like this secret. I was worried about telling Mom, but she gave me a hug to make me feel safe. We've never seen her friend again." Peter

"Am I safe when I go to school?"

As you grow up, you may be able to travel to school without your parents. If possible, walk with friends rather than alone. Avoid badly lit areas that may be deserted. Plan your route to pass busy places, such as a library or police station, where you could go for help if necessary.

It's best to travel to school with one or more friends.

School is a place of fun, learning, and safety. Teachers are there to teach and look after you, but you can also help keep yourself safe.

Say "no" and walk away if you ever feel under pressure to behave in a way that makes you feel uncomfortable.

My Story

"I went to school in my favorite sneakers but someone stole them while I was playing soccer. I felt so miserable about it. I'm not taking any of my best stuff to school again—it's not worth it." Carl

"How can I stay safe from bullying?"

Treating someone unkindly because of his or her skin color or religion is not ok. Picking on someone who is in some way different or seems an easy target is not ok. This is bullying and it should never be tolerated.

Support a friend if he or she is being bullied.

Speak out about bullying. Tell a teacher or a grown-up who can help. If you notice someone is being bullied, make an effort to be friendly to him or her.

Think about it

Dealing with bullying is not easy, but these tips may help.

- Walk away if possible.
- Don't fight back—you may get hurt.
- Be assertive—speak loudly and clearly.
- Tell someone you trust. If the bullying continues, you may need a grown-up to help.
- Do things that make you feel good about yourself. The more confident you feel, the easier it will be to deal with the bullying.

"Can I take risks?"

Life would be very dull if we never tried new things or took some risks. For instance, the first time you ride a bike you may fall off.

But getting on a bike for the first time without a helmet or hurtling down a steep hill is just dangerous. Only you can be a judge of danger.

Swimming is fun but water can be dangerous. Be aware of your abilities and judge risks sensibly.

It is always better to be safe than sorry. Now that you are aware of possible dangers, think about how you can prevent accidents and how to avoid or deal with dangerous situations you may face. Discuss the topics in this book with your parents or carers and agree what steps you can take to keep safe.

Think about it

What happens to your body when you feel unsafe and you just know that something isn't right? Some people get butterflies in their stomach. Others get goose bumps. These feelings help us stay away from danger. If you have a feeling like this, walk away from the situation and go to a safe place.

"What can I do?"

Follow these top safety tips for keeping safe:

• Think ahead.

• Don't panic. Breathe slowly.

• If you are in danger, shout!

• Say NO! to strangers.

• Don't give out personal information online.

• Learn your phone number.

• Avoid dark, deserted places.

• Speak out about trouble.

• Let a grown-up know if you see anything suspicious.

• If anyone ever does anything to make you feel unsafe, no matter who it is, walk away and tell a grown-up you trust.

Rules are there to keep you safe. Talk to your parents or carers about your rules for keeping safe.

Books on safety

If you want to read more about safety, try:

Let's Talk About Bullying
by Bruce Sanders (Stargazer)
Let's Talk About Drugs
by Sarah Levete (Stargazer)
Let's Talk About Alcohol
by Sarah Levete (Stargazer)

On the Web

These websites are also helpful:

www.fbi.gov/kids/6th12th/6th12th
www.suzylamplugh.org/smartkids
www.usfa.fema.gov/kids
www.childnet-int.org
www.kids.getnetwise.org
www.nhtsa.dot.gov/kids/
www.sass.ca

There is lots of useful information about safety on the internet.

Contact information

If you want to talk to someone who doesn't know you, these organizations can help:

NetSmartz Workshop
Charles B. Wang International
 Children's Building
699 Prince Street
Alexandria,
Virginia 22314-3175 USA
Freephone: 1-800-843-5678
www.netsmartz.org

Safe Kids Canada
2105-180 Dundas Street West
Toronto, ON M5G 1Z8
Canada
Tel: (416) 813-7288
www.safekids.ca/

Safe Kids USA
1301 Pennsylvania
Ave., NW
Suite 1000
Washington, DC
20004-1707, USA
Tel: (202) 662-0600
www.usa.safekids.org

Teens, Crime, and the Community
c/o National Crime Prevention Council
1000 Connecticut Ave., NW, 13th Floor
Washington, DC 20036, USA
Tel: (202) 466-6272
www.nationaltcc.org

Index

Photocredits
The publishers would like to acknowledge that the photographs reproduced in this book have been posed by models or have been obtained from photographic agencies.
Abbreviations: l-left, r-right, b-bottom, t-top, c-center, m-middle: Front cover, 12, 13tl, 25bl, 26 – Brand X Pictures. 1, 3mr, 25tr, 30 – DAJ Digital Images. 2, 21 – Iconotec. 3tr, 7tl, 8, 20, 27 – Corbis. 3br, 4. 9, 10, 18 – RP. 5, 14, 16, 19br – Comstock. 6, 24, 28 – Photodisc. 7br – PBD. 11 – Simon Morse. 13br – Image 100. 15, 17br, 19tl, 22, 23 – Digital Vision. 17tl – Getty Images. 29 – istockphoto.

Mount Laurel Library
100 Walt Whitman Avenue
Mount Laurel, NJ 08054-9539
856-234-7319
www.mtlaurel.lib.nj.us